Very
CRANBERRY

Very CRANBERRY

JENNIFER TRAINER THOMPSON

Celestial Arts
Berkeley | Toronto

Celestial Arts
an imprint of Ten Speed Press
P. O. Box 7123
Berkeley, California 94707
www.tenspeed.com

Distributed in Australia by Simon and Schuster Australia, in Canada by Ten Speed Press Canada, in New Zealand by Southern Publishers Group, in South Africa by Real Books, and in the United Kingdom and Europe by Publishers Group UK.

Cover and text design by Susanne Weihl

Library of Congress Cataloging-in-Publication Data
Thompson, Jennifer Trainer.
   Very cranberry / Jennifer Trainer Thompson.
     p. cm.
   ISBN-13: 978-1-58761-180-3 (pbk.)
   ISBN-10: 1-58761-180-5 (pbk.)
   1. Cookery (Cranberries) I. Title.
  TX813.C7T48 2003
  641.6′476—dc21   2003013312

Printed in Singapore

4 5 6 7 8 9 10—10 09 08

Acknowledgments

A special thanks to Linda Stripp for her culinary contribution, to Jody Fijal (tester extraordinaire), and to Lynn Danahy, who came up with the idea of a cranberry cookbook.

Contents

We have from the time called May until Michaelmas a great store of very good wild fruits as strawberries, cranberries and hurtleberries. The cranberries, much like cherries for color and bigness, may be kept until fruit comes in again. An excellent sauce is made of them for venison, turkeys and other great fowl and they are better to make tarts than either gooseberries or cherries. We have them brot to our homes by the Indians in great plenty.

—N. J. Mahon Stacy of New Jersey,
to his brother in England, on April 26, 1680

Introduction

Of all the books I've written, this one is closest to my heart, or at least my history. I grew up in cranberry country. As my dad would put it, I'm a bog-trotting swamp Yankee, which means a Yankee who grew up among the bogs and swamps of coastal southeastern Massachusetts. As a child, I skated with friends on the cranberry bogs in the winter. Our town's street signs weren't regulation green: they were cranberry colored, in a nod to the cranberry growers in the region. Riding my bike to town, I'd take shortcuts through the woods and along the sandy paths that ran between the square-cut bogs. It was a low-lying landscape of nineteenth-century lighthouses, tall white church steeples, the ospreys that gave Buzzard's Bay its name, and bogs.

Nearby is Plymouth, where Native Americans introduced the Pilgrims to cranberries in the mid-1600s. Native Americans already knew about the cranberry's versatility; by the time colonists arrived, Native Americans were eating cranberries, dyeing blankets and other fabrics with them, and using them to create a poultice for arrow wounds (believing cranberries to have healing powers). To Native Americans, cranberries were also symbolic; when tribes gathered to feast, the berries were served as a gesture of friendship and peace. Indeed, this indigenous fruit, which grows on vines and thrives in the sandy wetlands of southeastern Massachusetts. was served at the Pilgrim's first Thanksgiving feast with Chief Massasoit. (Cranberry sauce first made its published appearance in *The Pilgrim's Cook Book* of 1663.) Various tribes ascribed different names to the berry (the Cape Cod Pequots called it *ibimi* or "bitter berry"), while the Pilgrims dubbed the fruit "cranberry," because the shape of its blossom reminded them of the head and bill of a sandhill crane.

With so much history and staying power, perhaps it's not surprising that cranberries are also incredibly good for you, rich in fiber, vitamins, and phytochemicals that act as antioxidants and may promote good health. Early on, Native Americans taught New England colonists about the health benefits of this fruit; sailors took cranberries to sea with them, packing them in wooden barrels on the whaling expeditions of the 1800s and explorations to China to get a healthy dose of vitamin C and stave off scurvy (just as the English took limes and Spanish sailors took chiles for the same reason).

When you mention cranberries today, most people think of Thanksgiving, and the glistening ruby-colored sauce that's often served (ours always jiggled) in a cut-crystal bowl with a sterling silver spoon at Thanksgiving. And while I always look forward to the holiday and its traditional culinary trimmings, I've also discovered that the cranberry is a versatile and delectable ingredient. Not only that, the color is amazing: a deep, impenetrable garnet jewel that adds a majestic brushstroke of color and suggestion to many dishes. Don't relegate cranberries to the fall harvest; serve them year-round. Throughout these pages cranberries create a startling counterpoint to other flavors (Chipotle Cranberry Cornbread), take center stage and enliven basic recipes (Cranberry Turnovers), make terrific house gifts (Cranberry Blueberry Jam) and create fantastic desserts (Drenched Cranberry Cake). You'll find recipes using fresh or frozen as well as dried cranberries; fresh berries are available in stores throughout the fall and early winter and can be frozen for another month or so, and dried cranberries are available year-round. So serve them up, as Native Americans did, as a gesture of peace and friendship.

O ruddier than the cherry,
O sweeter than the berry,
O Nymph more bright
Than moonshine night,
Like kidlings blithe and merry.

—John Gay, *Acis and Galatea*

Salads and Starters

Almond Chicken and Cranberry Empanadas

You can prepare these turnovers, then freeze and cook them later. If you do so, simply add a few minutes to the baking time.

Dough

> 2 cups all-purpose flour
>
> 1 teaspoon salt
>
> $3/4$ cup (1 $1/2$ sticks) cold unsalted butter, cut into small dice
>
> $1/2$ cup cold water

Filling

> $3/4$ cup fresh or frozen cranberries
>
> 3 tablespoons water
>
> 2 tablespoons honey
>
> 2 tablespoons canola oil
>
> $1/2$ cup yellow onion, finely chopped
>
> 1 (6-ounce) boneless, skinless chicken breast half, finely chopped
>
> 10 oil-cured black olives, pitted and finely chopped
>
> 1 teaspoon ground cumin
>
> 1 teaspoon minced canned chipotle chile in adobo sauce
>
> 2 tablespoons minced fresh cilantro
>
> $1/4$ cup sliced almonds, toasted
>
> 1 tablespoon unsalted butter
>
> 1 egg beaten with 1 teaspoon water

To make the dough, combine the flour, salt, and butter in a food processor. Pulse to combine until the mixture resembles coarse cornmeal. With the machine running, gradually add the cold water until a dough forms. Remove the dough from the machine, wrap in plastic wrap, and refrigerate for 30 minutes.

To make the filling, combine the cranberries, water, and honey in a small saucepan and cook over medium-high heat for 5 minutes, stirring frequently. Remove from the heat and set aside.

In a large skillet, heat the oil over medium heat. Add the onion and sauté for 3 to 5 minutes, or until soft. Stir in the chicken, olives, cumin, chipotle, cilantro, almonds, butter, and cranberry mixture. Cook for 10 minutes, stirring frequently. Remove from the heat and let cool.

Position an oven rack in the center of the oven and preheat the oven to 400 F. Roll the dough out on a floured surface to a $\frac{1}{8}$-inch thickness. Using a cookie cutter or bowl, cut out rounds approximately 5 inches in diameter. Brush the perimeter with the egg mixture. Place a scant $\frac{1}{4}$ cup filling in the center of a round. Fold in half and crimp the edges with a fork. Repeat the process to use the remaining pastry and filling. Brush the tops of the empanadas with egg mixture. Place the empanadas on a nonstick baking pan and bake for 20 minutes, or until golden brown.

Serves 4

Seared Sea Scallops with Cranberry-Lime Sauce

This easy dish will make your friends think they are eating restaurant food. Be sure to check the scallops and remove the connector muscle.

Cranberry-Lime Sauce

> 2 tablespoons unsalted butter
> 3 tablespoons minced shallots
> $\frac{1}{4}$ teaspoon kosher salt
> $\frac{1}{4}$ cup coarsely chopped fresh or frozen cranberries
> $\frac{1}{3}$ cup cranberry juice
> $\frac{1}{4}$ teaspoon minced lime zest
> $\frac{1}{2}$ cup heavy cream

> 16 medium-to-large sea scallops
> Salt and freshly ground black pepper
> 1 tablespoon canola oil
> $\frac{1}{2}$ teaspoon unsalted butter
> Minced fresh chives or finely shredded lime zest, for garnish

To make the sauce, melt the butter in a small sauté pan over medium heat. Add the shallots and salt. Sauté for 2 minutes or until translucent. Add the cranberries, juice, and lime zest. Increase heat to medium-high and simmer for 5 minutes. Add the heavy cream and cook for 2 minutes. Remove from the heat and let cool slightly. In a blender, purée the mixture until smooth. Return to the saucepan, cover, and keep warm over very low heat.

Pat the scallops dry with paper towels and season generously with salt and pepper. Heat the oil in a large nonstick skillet over medium-high heat. Add the scallops and cook for 1 minute. Add the butter to the pan and cook for 2 more minutes, or until the scallops are browned. Turn the scallops over and cook for 2 to 3 minutes, or until browned on the second side. Using a slotted metal spatula, transfer to paper towels to drain. Place 1 tablespoon of cranberry-lime sauce on the center of each of 4 plates. Divide the scallops among the plates and garnish with chives.

Serves 4

Crab Cakes with Cranberry-Lemon Aioli

Panko are coarse Japanese bread crumbs, which can be found in Asian markets.

Aioli

> $1/4$ cup fresh or frozen cranberries, coarsely chopped
>
>   2 tablespoons sugar
>
>   2 to 3 tablespoons water
>
>   4 cloves minced garlic
>
>   2 tablespoons freshly squeezed lemon juice
>
>   1 teaspoon kosher salt
>
>   2 egg yolks
>
> $1/2$ cup extra virgin olive oil

Crab Cakes

>   8 ounces fresh lump crabmeat, or thawed frozen crabmeat
>
> $1/4$ cup panko or dried bread crumbs
>
>   1 tablespoon minced shallot
>
>   1 tablespoon minced chives
>
>   1 teaspoon Dijon mustard
>
> $1/4$ teaspoon minced lemon zest
>
>   3 tablespoons mayonnaise, preferably homemade
>
> $1/2$ teaspoon salt
>
>   1 egg, lightly beaten
>
>   3 tablespoons canola oil

To make the aioli, combine the cranberries, sugar, and 2 tablespoons water in a small saucepan. Bring to a boil, reduce heat to medium, and cook for 10 minutes, or until the cranberries have popped and the mixture has thickened. Remove from the heat and set aside to cool.

In a food processor, combine the garlic, lemon juice, salt, cranberry mixture, and egg yolks. Process until smooth. With the machine running, drizzle in olive oil and process until thick and creamy. (Add the 1 tablespoon water to thin, if necessary.) Transfer to a bowl and set aside.

To make the crab cakes, preheat the oven to 400 F. In a small bowl, combine the crabmeat and panko. Stir to blend. In a medium bowl, combine the shallot, chives, mustard, lemon zest, mayonnaise, salt, and egg. Fold in the crabmeat mixture to blend. (The uncooked crab mixture can be covered and refrigerated for up to 6 hours.) Shape into 4 cakes. In a large ovenproof skillet, heat the oil over medium-high heat. Add the crab cakes and cook for 2 to 3 minutes on each side, or until golden brown. Transfer the pan to the oven and bake for 10 minutes. Serve immediately, with the aioli.

Serves 4

Cranberry Poached Pear Salad with Brie and Pancetta

The saltiness of pancetta is an excellent balance to the mild flavor of Brie. You could also substitute Stilton cheese for the Brie, as Stilton pairs well with poached pears; if you do so, just omit the pancetta and garnish the salad with toasted walnuts.

$^1\!/_2$ cup Merlot wine

$^1\!/_2$ cup cranberry juice

2 tablespoons sugar

$^1\!/_2$ cup fresh or frozen cranberries, coarsely chopped in a
food processor

2 firm, ripe Bosc pears, peeled and halved lengthwise

4 ounces pancetta, cut into $^1\!/_2$-inch dice

2 ounces Brie cheese, cut into 4 pieces

1 small head curly endive, washed and chopped into
bite-sized pieces

2 tablespoons olive oil or walnut oil

1 tablespoon freshly squeezed lemon juice

Salt

In a medium saucepan, combine the Merlot, cranberry juice, sugar, and cranberries. Bring to a boil over high heat, stirring to dissolve the sugar. Cut the rounded side from the pears so they lie flat. Add the pears to the saucepan and reduce the heat to medium. Simmer for 10 minutes, turn the pears over, and cook 10 minutes longer, or until tender when pierced with a knife. Remove from the heat and let cool in the liquid. Using a slotted spoon, transfer the pears to a plate.

Remove and discard 1 cup of the poaching liquid from the saucepan. Add the remaining liquid to the blender and purée until smooth. Return to the pan and simmer over medium-high heat for 10 minutes, or until the liquid is syrupy enough to coat the back of a spoon. Remove from the heat and set aside.

Preheat the oven to 400 F. Put the pancetta on a small, sided baking sheet and bake for 20 minutes, or until crisp. Remove from the oven and let cool.

Preheat the broilers. Place the pears on a small baking sheet. Place 1 piece of Brie in the hollow of each pear and broil 2 inches under the heat source for 2 minutes, or until the the cheese is melted. Remove from the oven.

In a large bowl, combine the endive, lemon juice, oil, and salt. Toss well.

Divide the greens among 4 plates. Place a pear in the center of the greens. Drizzle 1 tablespoon of the reduced poaching liquid over each pear. Sprinkle with pancetta and serve.

Serves 4

Lentil Salad with Walnuts, Cranberries, and Feta Cheese

Served with a green salad or over greens, this salad makes a nice first course or light lunch entrée. The flavors of the salad develop as time passes, so let it sit for at least 15 minutes before serving.

> $3/4$ cup green French lentils
> 1 teaspoon minced garlic
> 2 tablespoons minced shallots
> 1 teaspoon kosher salt
> $1/4$ cup walnuts, toasted and chopped
> $1/4$ cup dried cranberries
> $1/4$ cup crumbled feta cheese
> 1 tablespoon freshly squeezed lemon juice
> 1 tablespoon red wine or cider vinegar
> 1 tablespoon extra virgin olive oil
> Salt and freshly ground black pepper

Rinse and pick over the lentils. In a small saucepan, combine the lentils and water to cover plus 2 inches. Add the garlic, shallots, and salt. Bring to a boil, reduce the heat to medium, and simmer for 25 minutes, or until tender but firm. Drain. Add the walnuts, cranberries, feta, lemon juice, vinegar, and olive oil. Blend well. Season with salt and pepper.

Serves 2

Cranberry Vinegar

With its clean, crisp flavor, this vinegar is a delicious alternative to balsamic vinegar in your salad dressing. Add the cranberries to the bottle and you have a beautiful house gift.

　　1 cup fresh or frozen cranberries, plus extra for bottle
　　2 tablespoons sugar
　　2 cups distilled white vinegar

In a medium saucepan, combine all the ingredients. Bring to a boil. Remove from the heat and let stand for 1 hour. Strain through a fine-mesh sieve lined with cheesecloth and placed over a bowl. Using a funnel, pour the vinegar into a clean bottle. Add a few berries. Stopper and store in the refrigerator for up to 1 month.

Makes 2 cups

Goat Cheese Tart with Cranberry-Onion Confit

This confit is delicious with filet mignon or sirloin steak. For variety, you can also add fresh thyme, chives, basil, or green onions to the tart filling, or garlic or herbs to the crust.

Tart Shell

    1 cup all-purpose flour

    1 $^1\!/_2$ tablespoons vegetable shortening

    $^1\!/_4$ cup cold unsalted butter, cut into small pieces

    $^1\!/_2$ teaspoon salt

    3 tablespoons ice water

Cranberry-Onion Confit

    2 tablespoons unsalted butter

    2 cups thinly sliced yellow onions

    3 teaspoons sugar

    1 teaspoon salt

    $^1\!/_4$ cup balsamic vinegar

    $^1\!/_2$ cup fresh or frozen cranberries, coarsely chopped

Filling

    5 $^1\!/_2$ ounces soft goat cheese

    1 cup heavy cream

    1 teaspoon kosher salt

    3 eggs

To make the tart shell, combine the flour, shortening, butter, and salt in a food processor. Pulse until the mixture resembles coarse cornmeal. With the machine running, gradually add the water until a dough forms. On a lightly floured surface, form the dough into ball. Press into a disk, wrap in plastic wrap, and refrigerate for 30 minutes.

Remove the dough from the refrigerator. On a lightly floured surface, roll the dough out to a $\frac{1}{8}$-inch thickness. Fit the dough into a 9-inch springform tart pan and trim the edges.

To make the confit, melt the butter over medium heat in a medium, heavy skillet. Add the onions, sprinkle with sugar and salt and cook, stirring occasionally, for 15 minutes. Add the vinegar and cranberries and simmer for 10 minutes, or until most of the liquid has evaporated. Remove from heat and set aside.

Adjust an oven rack in the middle of the oven. Preheat the oven to 375 F. To make the filling, combine the goat cheese, heavy cream, and salt in a food processor. Blend until smooth. With the machine running, add the eggs one at a time.

Pour the filling into the tart shell. Bake until the center is golden and firm, about 30 minutes. Remove from the oven. Remove the rim from the pan and cut the tart into 8 wedges. Serve hot, with a spoonful of confit on each wedge.

Serves 8

Watercress and Belgian Endive Salad
with Great Hill Blue Cheese and Cranberry Vinaigrette

The Great Hill Dairy is a small family-owned farm on the majestic Stone Estate, located on Buzzard's Bay in southeastern Massachusetts. This is also cranberry country, and you'll find that the fruit's strong flavor pairs well with Great Hill blue cheese, or another sharp, crumbly blue cheese, and watercress. If you like, add the chopped mint to the vinaigrette. This salad goes well with the salmon on page 36.

Cranberry Vinaigrette

>   2 teaspoons minced shallots
> $\frac{1}{8}$ teaspoon Dijon mustard
> $\frac{1}{8}$ teaspoon minced garlic
>   1 teaspoon sugar
>   2 tablespoons cranberry juice
> $\frac{1}{8}$ teaspoon kosher salt
>   2 tablespoons fresh or frozen cranberries
>   1 tablespoon cider vinegar
> $\frac{1}{4}$ cup canola oil

>   Leaves from 1 head Belgian endive
>   2 bunches watercress (about 4 ounces each), stemmed
>   Salt
> $\frac{1}{2}$ cup crumbled sharp blue cheese, preferably Great Hill Blue

To make the vinaigrette, combine the shallot, mustard, garlic, sugar, cranberry juice, salt, cranberries, and vinegar in a blender. With the machine running, gradually add the oil in a thin stream to make an emulsified sauce.

Cut the endive spears into thin crosswise strips. In a large bowl, combine the endive and watercress. Add the vinaigrette and toss to coat. Add the salt and toss again. Place a mound of salad greens on each of 4 to 6 plates and sprinkle with blue cheese.

Serves 4 to 6

Well, art is art, isn't it? Still, on the other hand, water is water! And east is east and west is west and if you take cranberries and stew them like applesauce they taste much more like prunes than rhubarb does.

—Groucho Marx

Side Dishes

Spaghetti Squash with Cinnamon and Cranberries

This simple dish is a tasty addition to the Thanksgiving table.

$1/2$ spaghetti squash, seeds and strings removed
1 cup water
1 teaspoon kosher salt
3 tablespoons firmly packed brown sugar
$1/2$ teaspoon cinnamon
2 tablespoons unsalted butter, cut into small pieces
$1/2$ cup fresh or frozen cranberries
1 tablespoon maple syrup

Preheat the oven to 400 F. Place the squash, flesh side down, in a baking dish. Add 1 inch of water and bake for 40 minutes, or until soft and easily pierced with a fork. Remove from the oven and let cool to the touch. Scrape out the interior with a fork into a casserole dish. Stir in the salt, brown sugar, cinnamon, butter, and cranberries. Cover and return to the oven for 25 minutes. Remove from the oven, drizzle maple syrup over the top, and stir well. Serve warm.

Serves 4

Acorn Squash Stuffed with Curried Apples, Onions, and Cranberries

Curry adds a nice flavor twist to three fall ingredients: apples, onions, and cranberries.

1 acorn squash, halved lengthwise and seeded

2 teaspoons maple syrup

1 teaspoon kosher salt

1 tablespoon plus 1 teaspoon unsalted butter

$1/2$ cup chopped yellow onion

1 teaspoon curry powder

1 large Granny Smith apple, peeled, cored, and cut into $1/2$-inch dice

$1/4$ cup dried cranberries

Preheat the oven to 400 F. Cut the rounded bottom off each acorn squash so they will lie flat on a baking sheet. Rub 1 teaspoon maple syrup over the flesh side of each squash. Sprinkle each with $1/4$ teaspoon salt. Place on a baking sheet, flesh side up, and roast for 30 minutes

In a skillet, melt the 1 tablespoon butter over medium heat. Add the onion and cook for 2 minutes. Add the curry powder and the remaining $1/2$ teaspoon salt and continue to cook for 2 minutes. Add the apple and cranberries cook for 2 more minutes. Remove from the heat and set aside.

Divide the apple mixture between the squash halves. Top each with $1/2$ teaspoon butter and place in a large casserole dish. Cover with aluminum foil and bake for 30 to 45 minutes, or until tender when pierced with a fork.

Serves 2

Quinoa with Cranberries, Pistachios, and Thyme

High in protein, with an essential amino acid balance, quinoa has been called the world's most perfect food. An ancient grain that originated in the Andes Mountains, it was a staple food of the Inca civilization.

1 tablespoon unsalted butter
$^1{}_2$ cup finely chopped onion
1 cup quinoa, rinsed
1 $^1{}_2$ cups chicken or vegetable stock
1 tablespoon chopped fresh thyme
$^1{}_2$ cup dried cranberries
1 teaspoon salt
$^1{}_2$ cup pistachios, coarsely chopped

In a small saucepan, melt the butter over medium heat. Add the onion and sauté until soft, about 3 minutes. Stir in the quinoa and stir for 2 minutes to toast. Add the chicken stock and bring to a boil. Reduce heat to a simmer; add the thyme, cranberries, and salt. Cover and cook for 15 minutes, or until all the liquid is absorbed. Stir in the pistachios and serve hot.

Serves 4

Lemon-Scented Couscous with Cranberries and Pine Nuts

A tasty accompaniment to roast chicken or pork.

> 1 $\frac{3}{4}$ cups chicken stock
> 2 tablespoons freshly squeezed lemon juice
> 1 tablespoon unsalted butter
> $\frac{3}{4}$ teaspoon kosher salt
> 1 $\frac{1}{2}$ cups couscous
> $\frac{1}{4}$ cup dried cranberries
> $\frac{1}{2}$ teaspoon minced lemon zest
> $\frac{1}{4}$ cup pine nuts, toasted

In a medium saucepan, combine the chicken stock, lemon juice, butter, and salt. Bring to a boil. Stir in the couscous and cranberries. Remove from the heat, cover, and let sit for 10 minutes, or until the stock is absorbed. Remove the lid and fluff the couscous with a fork. Stir in the lemon zest and pine nuts. Serve immediately.

Serves 4 to 6

Festive Wild Rice

This is an excellent accompaniment to pheasant or venison.

    2 beets
    4 cups plus 2 tablespoons water
    1 cup $\frac{1}{2}$-inch-diced sugar pumpkin or butternut squash
    1 tablespoon canola oil
    1 teaspoon salt, plus additional for sprinkling
    $\frac{1}{2}$ cup wild rice
    $\frac{1}{2}$ cup brown rice
    $\frac{1}{2}$ cup dried cranberries
    4 green onions, minced
    2 tablespoons minced fresh mint, finely chopped
    1 tablespoon red wine vinegar
    1 tablespoon extra virgin olive oil
    Freshly ground black pepper

Preheat the oven to 400 F. Place the beets in a small baking pan with the 2 tablespoons of water. Cover and roast until the beets can be easily pierced with fork, 40 to 50 minutes. Remove from the oven and let cool. Peel and cut into $\frac{1}{2}$-inch dice. Set aside.

In a small bowl, toss the pumpkin with the canola oil. Sprinkle with salt and place on a baking sheet. Roast for 15 to 20 minutes, or just until tender. Set aside.

In a medium saucepan, bring the 4 cups water and 1 teaspoon salt to a boil. Add the wild rice and brown rice, cover, and reduce heat to low. Simmer for 35 to 45 minutes. Drain and place in a medium bowl. Add the cranberries, beets, pumpkin, green onions, mint, vinegar, and olive oil. Season with salt and pepper. Serve at room temperature or chilled.

Makes 4 cups

Cranberry-Chestnut Stuffing with Oyster Mushrooms

This amount will stuff a 10- to 12-pound turkey.

10 chestnuts
6 tablespoons butter
1 cup finely chopped yellow onion
1 cup finely chopped celery
1 tablespoon canola oil
8 ounces oyster mushrooms, stemmed and torn into
    bite-sized pieces
Salt
1 cup chicken stock
5 cups bite-sized pieces French bread
1 tablespoon minced fresh sage
2 tablespoons minced fresh flat-leaf parsley
$\frac{1}{3}$ cup dried cranberries
Freshly ground black pepper

Preheat the oven to 450 F. Using a paring knife, cut an X into the round side of each nut. Place in the oven and roast for 10 minutes. Remove and let cool slightly. Peel the chestnuts while still warm. Chop finely.

Preheat the oven to 350 F. Melt 2 tablespoons of the butter in a medium sauté pan over medium-high heat. Add the onion and celery and sauté until soft, about 6 minutes. Remove from the heat and set aside.

Heat the oil in a sauté pan over medium-high heat. Add the oyster mushrooms and cook about 10 minutes, until golden brown on the edges. Transfer to paper towels to drain. Salt well. In a small saucepan, melt the remaining 4 tablespoons butter in the chicken stock.

In a large bowl, combine the chestnuts, onion, celery, mushrooms, French bread, herbs, and cranberries. Pour the chicken stock over the mixture and toss gently. Add salt and pepper to taste. To use as a dressing, place the stuffing in a baking dish, cover with aluminum foil, and bake until hot, 20 to 30 minutes. Remove the aluminum foil and bake another 5 to 10 minutes, or until crispy on top.

Makes 6 cups; serves 6

Whatever the regional differences,
one thing is constant all over the nation—the cranberry.
The red berry is jellied and cut in quivering slices, stewed and served with whole berries,
squeezed and poured into glasses as a cocktail; nationwide it is spiked with spirits, baked in
bread, chopped into a relish, embalmed in gelatin or cubed in a salad.

—Horace Sutton,
"The Cranberry Connection" in *Saturday Review*

Entrées

Braised Lamb Shanks with Sweet Garlic and Cranberry Jus

These lamb shanks are complemented by roasted yukon gold potatoes.

$1\!/\!2$ cup fresh or frozen cranberries
$1\!/\!4$ cup water
2 tablespoons sugar
2 (1-pound) lamb shanks
Salt and freshly ground black pepper
3 tablespoons canola oil
$1\!/\!2$ cup chopped onion
$3\!/\!4$ cup port
2 cups beef stock
4 cloves garlic, minced
1 tablespoon chopped fresh rosemary
1 tablespoon unsalted butter

Preheat the oven to 325 F. In small saucepan, combine the cranberries, water, and sugar. Bring to a boil, reduce heat to medium-low, and cook, stirring occasionally, for 10 minutes, or until the cranberries have popped and the mixture has thickened. Remove from the heat and set aside.

Pat the lamb shanks dry with paper towels. Season with salt and pepper. Heat the oil in a Dutch oven over high heat. Add the lamb and sear on all sides, browning well, about 8 minutes. Remove the shanks and reduce heat to medium. Add the onion and cook for 3 minutes, stirring. Stir in the port, stock, garlic, rosemary, and cranberry mixture. Cook for 5 minutes. Add the lamb shanks, cover, and braise in the oven for 1 hour. Turn the shanks over and continue cooking for 1 hour longer. Remove the lamb shanks from the oven. Transfer to a platter and cover with aluminum foil to keep warm. Transfer the Dutch oven to the stove top. Bring the braising liquid to a simmer over medium heat. Whisk in the butter. Simmer, stirring occasionally, for about 10 minutes, or until the liquid is slightly reduced. Serve the lamb shanks topped with the jus.

Serves 2

Seared Salmon with Cranberry-Mustard Vinaigrette

This recipe can't get any more healthful (and it tastes great too!). The salmon provides great omega-3 and -6 oils, while the cranberries contain significant amounts of antioxidants that help to prevent disease.

4 (6-ounce) boneless salmon fillets, pin bones removed
Salt and freshly ground white pepper
2 tablespoons canola oil

Cranberry-Mustard Vinaigrette

1 tablespoon minced shallot
$1/4$ teaspoon Dijon mustard
$1/4$ teaspoon dry mustard
$1/4$ cup fresh or frozen cranberries
$1/2$ teaspoon sugar
$1/4$ teaspoon kosher salt
2 tablespoons rice wine vinegar
$1/2$ cup extra virgin olive oil
$1/2$ teaspoon minced fresh thyme

To make the vinaigrette, combine the shallot, Dijon mustard, dry mustard, cranberries, sugar, salt, and rice wine vinegar in a blender or food processor. Mix well. With the machine running, gradually add the olive oil in a thin stream. Finally, add the thyme and pulse to combine.

Preheat the oven to 400 F. Pat the salmon dry with paper towels. Season generously on both sides with salt and pepper. In a large skillet, heat the canola oil over medium-high heat until almost smoking. Place the salmon in the pan, skin side up, and cook for 2 to 3 minutes, or until browned on the bottom. Turn the salmon over and cook for 2 minutes. Place the salmon on a baking sheet and roast in the oven for 3 to 5 minutes, or until barely translucent in the center. Serve hot, with vinaigrette spooned over.

Serves 4

Grilled Pork Chops with Cranberry-Apple Compote

This compote is good with roasted meats such as pork tenderloin or chicken. (It would also be fantastic with soft warm cheeses like Brie or pan-fried goat cheese.)

Cranberry-Apple Compote

> 1 tablespoon unsalted butter
> 1 small yellow onion, finely chopped
> Kosher salt
> $^1/_2$ teaspoon minced fresh ginger
> $^1/_2$ cup water
> 4 Granny Smith apples, peeled, cored, and finely chopped
> 2 tablespoons firmly packed brown sugar
> $^1/_2$ teaspoon ground cinnamon
> 1 cup fresh or frozen cranberries
>
> 4 (6-ounce) boneless pork chops
> Kosher salt and freshly ground black pepper

To make the compote, melt the butter in small saucepan over medium heat. Add the onion and sauté until translucent, about 3 minutes. Season with salt. Add the ginger and sauté for 2 more minutes. Add the water, apples, brown sugar, cinnamon, and cranberries. Cook, stirring occasionally, for 15 minutes over medium heat, or until thickened.

Prepare a hot fire in a charcoal grill or preheat a gas grill to medium high. Oil the grill rack. Pat the pork chops dry and season both sides generously with salt and pepper. Grill the chops for about 8 minutes on each side, or until barely pink in the center. Top each pork chop with a little warmed compote.

Serves 4

Pan-Seared Duck Breast with Cranberry-Ginger Relish

Properly cooked duck should be medium-rare, so don't be put off by the short cooking time.

Relish

> 1 cup fresh or frozen cranberries
> $1/2$ teaspoon grated orange zest
> $1/2$ teaspoon minced fresh ginger
> $1/4$ teaspoon kosher salt
> 2 tablespoons sugar
> 2 tablespoons freshly squeezed orange juice
> $1/2$ teaspoon honey

> 4 (6-ounce) boneless, skin-on duck breasts, patted dry
> $1/2$ teaspoon kosher salt
> $1/4$ teaspoon freshly ground black pepper
> 2 tablespoons canola oil

To make the relish, combine all the ingredients in a food processor. Process to a coarse purée. Use now, or cover and refrigerate for up to 3 days.

Adjust an oven rack in the top part of the oven. Preheat the oven to 400 F. Place the duck on a work surface skin side up. Using a sharp knife, score four $1/2$-inch-deep cuts across the skin at a

45-degree angle. Sprinkle the salt and pepper over the meat side of the duck breasts.

Heat the oil the in a large, heavy skillet over high heat until almost smoking. Add two duck breasts, skin side down, and cook for 5 minutes, or until brown and crisp on the bottom. Make sure the breasts don't touch each other. Turn and cook for 2 more minutes, or until browned on the second side. Remove the pan from the heat and transfer the duck breasts, skin side down, to a baking sheet. Repeat for the remaining two breasts. Roast in the oven on the top rack for 5 minutes. Remove from the oven and slice each breast into $^1/_4$-inch-thick diagonal strips. Fan out on warmed plates and spoon cranberry-ginger relish over the top. Serve immediately.

Serves 4

I

It has been an unchallengeable American doctrine that cranberry sauce, a pink goo with overtones of sugared tomatoes, is a delectable necessity of the Thanksgiving board and that turkey is uneatable without it. . . . There are some things in every country that you must be born to endure; and another hundred years of general satisfaction with Americans and America could not reconcile this expatriate to cranberry sauce, peanut butter, and drum majorettes.

—Alistair Cooke, *Talk about America*

Holiday Relishes and Gifts

Cranberry Salsa

A salsa that's good with grilled shrimp, meats, or chicken. It's also excellent as an accompaniment to sweet potato fries, and an interesting twist on a post-Thanksgiving turkey sandwich.

- $\frac{1}{2}$ cup dried cranberries
- $\frac{1}{2}$ cup boiling water
- $\frac{1}{2}$ cup fresh or frozen cranberries
- 2 tablespoons cold water
- 2 serrano chiles, minced, or $\frac{1}{2}$ teaspoon minced habanero chile
- $\frac{1}{4}$ cup finely chopped red onion
- 2 tablespoons minced fresh cilantro
- 1 tablespoon freshly squeezed lime juice

Place the dried cranberries in a small bowl. Pour the water over the cranberries. Let sit for 10 minutes. Drain, reserving the water. In a food processor, combine the soaked cranberries, the fresh or frozen cranberries, the 2 tablespoons water, and the chiles. Pulse until finely chopped and well mixed. Place in a small bowl and stir in the red onion, cilantro, and lime juice. Cover and store in the refrigerator for up to 4 days.

Makes 1 cup

Mary Jane's Cranberry Relish

A crowd pleaser every time, this recipe from my mother-in-law takes minutes to make and will keep for weeks. The flavors improve with age.

- 3 cups fresh or frozen cranberries
- 1 unpeeled orange, scrubbed, quartered, and seeded
- 1 apple, quartered and cored
- 1 cup sugar

Combine all the ingredients in food processor. Pulse to a purée. Transfer to a bowl. Serve now, or cover and refrigerate for up to 1 month.

Makes 3 cups

Cranberry-Pineapple Relish

Combining tart, sweet, and hot flavors, this relish is a bright garnish for grilled meats, fish, or quesadillas. It will keep in the refrigerator for 4 days, but the heat of the pepper will be lost after the first day, due to the acidity of the cranberry and pineapple.

- $\frac{1}{4}$ cup finely chopped red onion
- 1 cup finely chopped fresh or frozen cranberries
- 1 $\frac{1}{2}$ cups finely diced fresh pineapple
- 2 teaspoons minced jalapeño chiles
- 2 teaspoons honey
- 1 tablespoon minced fresh mint
- $\frac{1}{2}$ teaspoon chile powder
- 1 tablespoon freshly squeezed lime juice
- $\frac{1}{4}$ teaspoon salt

Combine all the ingredients in a medium bowl. Let sit at room temperature for 30 minutes before serving. Cover and store in the refrigerator for up to 4 days.

Makes 2 cups

Cranberry-Horseradish Sauce

This is a great condiment on almost all meats: ham, pork, chicken, and beef. It's even good with seafood.

- 1 tablespoon unsalted butter
- $\frac{1}{4}$ cup finely chopped onion
- $\frac{1}{4}$ teaspoon kosher salt
- 1 cup chopped fresh or frozen cranberries
- $\frac{1}{4}$ cup sugar
- $\frac{1}{2}$ cup water
- $\frac{1}{4}$ cup prepared horseradish
- 1 teaspoon Dijon mustard

In a small saucepan, melt the butter over medium heat. Add the onions and sauté for 5 minutes, or until golden. Sprinkle with the salt and stir. Add the cranberries, sugar, and water. Stir to combine. Cook for 15 minutes, or until thickened. Remove from the heat. Stir in the horseradish and mustard until blended. Serve at room temperature or chilled. Store in the refrigerator, covered, for up to 1 week.

Makes 1 cup

Cranberry Sauce

During Thanksgiving week, Americans eat 80 million pounds of cranberries, partly due to tradition but also because they taste great with turkey. This sauce is easy to make and keeps well. The cranberry butter that follows is a great spread for hot corn bread or other baked goods.

^{1}2 cup water

1 ^{1}2 cups sugar

^{1}4 cup dry red wine

4 cups fresh or frozen cranberries

In a large saucepan, bring the water and sugar to a boil. Reduce the heat and simmer for 5 minutes. Add the red wine and cranberries. Continue cooking, stirring occasionally, for 10 minutes, or until thickened. Remove from the heat and let cool. Serve now, or cover and refrigerate for up to 2 weeks.

Makes 3 cups

Cranberry Butter: In a medium bowl, combine ^{1}2 cup of the above sauce with ^{1}2 cup (1 stick) unsalted butter at room temperature. Blend with a rubber spatula until well combined.

Spiced Cranberry-Apricot Sauce

Serve this sauce with Thanksgiving turkey or a roast pork loin.

$1/2$ cup sugar
$1/4$ cup water
$1/2$ teaspoon ground cinnamon
$1/2$ teaspoon ground cardamom
$1/4$ teaspoon freshly grated nutmeg
$1/2$ cup apricot preserves
1 cup fresh or frozen cranberries
$1/4$ cup dried apricots, chopped

In a small saucepan, combine the sugar, water, cinnamon, cardamom, and nutmeg. Bring to a boil. Add the preserves, cranberries, and dried apricots. Reduce the heat to medium and cook for 10 minutes, stirring occasionally. Serve now, or let cool, cover, and refrigerate for up to 2 weeks.

Makes 1 $1/4$ cup

Cranberry Applesauce

This tastes like applesauce, with a bit of cranberry flavor and a beautiful color.

2 cups fresh or frozen cranberries
3 Granny Smith apples, peeled, cored, and cut into $\frac{1}{2}$-inch dice
3 Golden Delicious apples, peeled, cored, and cut into $\frac{1}{2}$-inch dice
$\frac{1}{4}$ cup water
$\frac{1}{4}$ cup cranberry juice
$\frac{2}{3}$ cup sugar
1 tablespoon honey

In a heavy saucepan, combine all the ingredients. Cook over medium heat, uncovered and stirring frequently, until the apples and cranberries are soft, about 15 minutes. Remove from the heat and let cool. Force through a medium-mesh sieve or food mill. Serve now, or cover and refrigerate for up to 1 week.

Makes 4 cups

Cranberry-Blueberry Jam

This jam is a hearty blend of two native American fruits. For holidays or birthdays, make a big batch to give away as gifts, adding a note that the Indians served cranberries as a gesture of peace and friendship.

2 cups fresh or frozen cranberries

2 cups fresh or frozen blueberries

3 cups sugar

$\frac{3}{4}$ cup water

In a large saucepan, combine all the ingredients and bring to a boil over high heat. Reduce the heat to medium-low and simmer, stirring occasionally, for 25 minutes, or until thickened. Pour into sterilized jars, seal, let cool, and refrigerate for up to 1 month.

Makes 4 cups

Cherry-Cranberry Conserve

This fabulous chunky spread is good on hearty breads, scones, or biscuits, or served as a relish with grilled chicken or meat.

    1 cup pitted, fresh sweet cherries
    2 cups fresh or frozen cranberries
    2 cups sugar
    $\frac{1}{4}$ cup freshly squeezed orange juice
    $\frac{1}{4}$ cup dried currants
    $\frac{1}{2}$ cup chopped walnuts

In a large saucepan, combine the cherries, cranberries, sugar, and juice. Bring to a boil. Reduce the heat to medium and simmer, stirring frequently, for 15 to 20 minutes, or until thickened. Stir in the currants and walnuts. Serve now, or pour into sterilized jars, seal, and refrigerate for up to 2 weeks.

Makes 3 cups

Cranberry-Orange Spread

Use this as an alternative to maple syrup for pancakes or French toast. It also makes a nice filling for dessert crêpes.

   2 cups fresh or frozen cranberries
   1 navel orange, peeled, seeded, and coarsely chopped
   2 cups sugar
   $\frac{1}{2}$ cup freshly squeezed orange juice

In a medium saucepan, combine all the ingredients and bring to a boil over high heat. Cover and reduce the heat to medium-low. Simmer for 15 minutes. Strain through a medium-mesh sieve, pressing on the solids with the back of a large spoon, or until thickened. Let cool and use now, or cover and refrigerate for up to 1 month.

Makes 2 cups

The morns are meeker than they were,

The nuts are getting brown;

The berry's cheek is plumper,

The rose is out of town.

—Emily Dickinson,
"The morns are meeker than they were"

Breads and Other Baked Goods

Cranberry-Chipotle Corn Bread

East meets West in this New England–Southwestern corn bread. It's best eaten warm with a little butter, and is a fantastic accompaniment to a Southwestern-style black bean soup or chili. Use leftover bread to make croutons or a Tex-Mex corn-bread stuffing.

I cup flour
I cup fine cornmeal
3 tablespoons sugar
3 teaspoons baking powder
I teaspoon salt
I cup fresh or frozen cranberries, coarsely chopped
2 eggs
I cup milk
3 tablespoons unsalted butter, melted
2 chipotle chiles in adobo sauce, minced
$\frac{1}{4}$ cup finely chopped green onions
2 tablespoons minced fresh cilantro

Preheat the oven to 400 F. Butter an 8-inch square baking pan. In a large bowl, combine the flour, cornmeal, sugar, baking powder, salt, and cranberries. Stir well to blend. In a medium bowl, beat the eggs, milk, and butter together until blended. Pour the wet ingredients into the dry and stir, just until combined, about 5 strokes. Add the chiles, green onions, and cilantro. Stir just enough to combine; the batter will be lumpy. Pour into the prepared pan and bake until golden brown and a toothpick inserted in the center comes out clean, about 30 minutes.

Serves 4 to 6

New England Biscuits with Cranberries and Rosemary

Biscuits are perfect for mopping up the turkey gravy at Thanksgiving or serving with soup on a cold winter day. To turn these into a hearty appetizer or snack, slice them in half, spread them with mayonnaise, and fill with sliced turkey.

2 cups all-purpose flour

2 $\frac{1}{2}$ teaspoons baking powder

2 teaspoons sugar

1 teaspoon salt

5 tablespoons cold unsalted butter, cut into small pieces

$\frac{1}{2}$ cup dried cranberries

2 tablespoons minced fresh rosemary, finely chopped

1 cup buttermilk

1 egg, lightly beaten

Preheat the oven to 400 F. Spray a baking sheet with vegetable-oil cooking spray or line it with parchment paper.

In a food processor, combine the flour, baking powder, sugar, and salt. Pulse to combine. Add the butter and process until the mixture resembles coarse cornmeal. Place the mixture in a large bowl. Stir in the cranberries, rosemary, and buttermilk. Mix well. The dough will be sticky. Transfer to a floured work surface. Dust your hands with flour and knead the dough about 10 times, or until smooth. Pat into a round about $\frac{1}{2}$ inch thick. Using a 2-inch round biscuit cutter or drinking glass, cut out biscuits and place on the prepared pan. Gather the scraps and repeat until all the dough is used. Brush the biscuit tops with the beaten egg. Bake until golden, about 15 minutes. Transfer to a wire rack and let cool slightly or completely.

Makes 14 biscuits

Cranberry Scones

Serve butter or marmalade with these scones.

2 cups all-purpose flour
1 teaspoon salt
2 tablespoons granulated sugar
1 teaspoon baking soda
2 teaspoons baking powder
$\frac{1}{2}$ cup (1 stick) cold unsalted butter, cut into small dice
$\frac{1}{2}$ cup dried cranberries
1 egg
$\frac{1}{2}$ cup plus 2 tablespoons heavy cream
$\frac{1}{4}$ cup turbinado sugar

Preheat the oven to 400 F. Spray a baking sheet with vegetable-oil cooking spray or line it with parchment paper.

In a food processor, combine the flour, salt, granulated sugar, and baking soda, baking powder; pulse to mix. Add the butter and pulse until the mixture resembles coarse cornmeal. Transfer to a large bowl and add the cranberries. In a small bowl, whisk the egg and the $\frac{1}{2}$ cup cream together until blended. Add to the dry ingredients and stir until a loose dough forms. On a lightly floured work surface, knead the dough gently, about 10 times, until smooth. Form a 6-inch round.

Cut the round into 8 wedges. Transfer the wedges to the prepared pan. Brush the tops with 2 tablespoons heavy cream and sprinkle with turbinado sugar. Bake for 15 minutes or until golden. Transfer to a wire rack and let cool slightly. Serve warm.

Makes 8 scones

Cranberry-Vanilla Sour Cream Coffee Cake

You could easily substitute blueberries for cranberries in this coffee cake.

Topping

- $1/4$ cup firmly packed brown sugar
- 3 tablespoons all-purpose flour
- 3 tablespoons cold unsalted butter, cut into small pieces

- 2 cups all-purpose flour
- 1 teaspoons baking powder
- 1 teaspoons baking soda
- $1/2$ teaspoon salt
- $1/2$ cup (1 stick) unsalted butter, at room temperature
- $1\ 1/4$ cups granulated sugar
- 3 eggs
- $1/4$ teaspoon vanilla extract
- $3/4$ cup sour cream
- 2 cups fresh or frozen cranberries

To make the topping, combine the brown sugar, flour, and cold butter in a food processor. Process just until crumbly.

Preheat the oven to 350 F. Spray an 8-inch springform pan lightly with vegetable-oil cooking spray.

In a medium bowl, combine the flour, baking powder, baking soda, and salt. Stir to blend well. In the bowl of an electric mixer on medium speed, cream the butter and granulated sugar together until light and fluffy. Add the eggs one at a time, beating thoroughly after each addition. Add the vanilla and sour cream. Blend until smooth. Gradually add the dry ingredients and beat until blended. Fold in the cranberries. Scrape the batter into the prepared pan. Sprinkle the top evenly with the topping. Bake for 60 minutes, or until a cake tester inserted in the center comes out clean. Let cool in the pan for 10 minutes. Release and remove the sides of the pan and transfer the cake to a wire rack to cool.

Makes 1 cake

Classic Cranberry Muffins

You can substitute blueberries for cranberries in this quintessential New England recipe.

I egg
$^1/_3$ cup canola oil
I cup buttermilk
I $^3/_4$ cups all-purpose flour
I cup sugar, plus additional for sprinkling
I teaspoon salt
2 teaspoons baking powder
$^1/_2$ teaspoon baking soda
I $^1/_2$ cups fresh or frozen cranberries, coarsely chopped
$^1/_2$ cup sliced almonds

Preheat the oven to 350°F. Spray 12 muffin cups with vegetable-oil cooking spray.

In a large bowl, combine the egg, oil, and buttermilk. Whisk to blend. In a medium bowl, combine the flour, sugar, salt, baking powder, and baking soda. Stir to blend well. Add the dry ingredients to the wet ingredients, stirring just until blended; the batter will be lumpy. Fold in the cranberries and almonds. Fill each prepared muffin cup three-fourths full with batter. Sprinkle each muffin with sugar. Bake for 25 minutes, or until an inserted toothpick comes out clean. Let cool for 5 minutes in the pan, then unmold onto wire racks.

Makes 12 muffins

Cranberry-Corn Muffins

The cranberries can be replaced by fresh or frozen blueberries, strawberries, or raspberries.

> 1 $\frac{1}{3}$ cups fresh or frozen cranberries
> $\frac{3}{4}$ cup plus 2 tablespoons sugar
> 1 cup yellow cornmeal
> 2 cups all-purpose flour
> $\frac{1}{2}$ teaspoon salt
> 1 $\frac{1}{2}$ teaspoons baking powder
> 2 teaspoons baking soda
> 2 eggs
> 1 cup milk
> $\frac{1}{2}$ cup (1 stick) unsalted butter, melted

Preheat the oven to 375 F. Spray 12 muffin cups with vegetable-oil cooking spray.

Rinse the cranberries, transfer to a small bowl, and sprinkle with the 2 tablespoons sugar. Set aside.

In a large bowl, combine the cornmeal, flour, salt, the $\frac{3}{4}$ cup sugar, the baking powder, baking soda, and cranberries. Stir to blend well. In a medium bowl, combine the eggs, milk, and butter. Whisk to blend. Make a well in the center of the dry ingredients. Add the wet ingredients and stir just until barely mixed; the batter will be lumpy. Fill the prepared muffin cups three-fourths full. Bake for 15 minutes, or until an inserted toothpick comes out clean. Let the muffins cool in the pan for 5 minutes, then unmold onto wire racks. Serve warm.

Makes 12 muffins

Cranberry-Nut Bread

The thick, crisp crust of this bread is what makes it so great. Use toasted walnuts if you don't have pecans. Using aluminum foil instead of plastic wrap helps to keep the crust crisp.

2 cups sifted all-purpose flour
1 cup sugar
1 $\frac{3}{4}$ teaspoons baking powder
1 teaspoon salt
$\frac{1}{2}$ teaspoon baking soda
1 egg
$\frac{1}{2}$ cup freshly squeezed orange juice
$\frac{1}{4}$ cup water
3 tablespoons unsalted butter, melted
2 cups fresh or frozen cranberries
1 cup pecans, toasted and chopped
1 teaspoon grated orange zest

Preheat the oven to 350 F. Line the bottom of an 8 by 4 by 3-inch loaf pan with waxed paper.

Sift the dry ingredients together into a large bowl. Make a well in the center. In a medium bowl, combine the egg, orange juice, water, and butter. Whisk to blend. Add the liquid ingredients to the dry ingredients and stir just until blended; the batter will be lumpy. Fold in the cranberries, nuts, and orange zest. Pour into the prepared pan and smooth the top.

Bake for 1 hour and 10 minutes, or until a tester inserted in the center comes out clean. Let cool on a wire rack. Unmold and remove the paper. Serve now, or wrap in aluminum foil and store for up to 3 days.

Makes 1 loaf

They sail'd to the Western Sea, they did,
To a land all cover'd with trees:
And they bought an owl, and a useful cart,
And a pound of rice, and a cranberry-tart

—Edward Lear, "The Jumblies"

Desserts

Chocolate Cranberry Biscotti

Served after dinner, these biscotti are delicious dipped in espresso, port, or rum.

   2 cups all-purpose flour
   $1/4$ cup unsweetened cocoa powder
   2 teaspoons baking powder
   $1/4$ teaspoon salt
   $1/4$ teaspoon ground cinnamon
   1 cup dried cranberries
   $1/2$ cup sliced almonds (optional)
   3 eggs
   1 cup sugar
   1 teaspoon vanilla extract
   8 ounces semisweet chocolate, chopped

Preheat the oven to 350 F. Lightly grease a baking sheet or line it with parchment paper.

In a large bowl, combine the flour, cocoa, baking powder, salt, and cinnamon. Stir well to blend. Stir in the cranberries and almonds. In another bowl, combine the eggs, sugar, and vanilla. Whisk until blended. Gradually stir in the dry ingredients until well blended. On a generously floured work surface, knead the dough with floured hands 4 or 5 times. Shape the dough into a flattened log about

12 inches long and 4 inches wide. Place on the prepared pan and bake for 30 minutes, or until firm to the touch. Remove from the oven and let cool to the touch on a wire rack. Transfer to a cutting board. Using a serrated knife, cut the loaf into $1/4$-inch-thick slices. Reduce the oven temperature to 300 F. Return the slices to the pan and bake for 10 minutes on each side, or until lightly crisped. Remove from the oven and let cool completely on wire racks.

Line a baking sheet with parchment paper. In a double boiler over barely simmering water, melt the chocolate. Stir until smooth. Dip each cookie halfway into the chocolate and place on the prepared pan. Refrigerate until the chocolate hardens, about 30 minutes.

Store in an airtight container in a cool, dry place for up to 1 week.

Makes 26 biscotti

Cranberry-Mango Mascarpone Tart

The mango's sweetness balances the sharp cranberry flavor, while the mascarpone gives the dessert depth and richness.

Tart Dough

> 1 $\frac{1}{4}$ cups all-purpose flour
> $\frac{1}{4}$ teaspoon salt
> 1 tablespoon sugar
> $\frac{1}{2}$ cup (1 stick) unsalted butter, cut into small pieces
> 4 tablespoons water

Filling

> 1 cup fresh or frozen cranberries
> $\frac{1}{4}$ cup water
> 1 $\frac{1}{2}$ cups sugar
> 4 eggs
> 8 ounces mascarpone cheese, at room temperature
> $\frac{1}{2}$ cup mango juice or purée
>
> Whipped cream, for serving

To make the dough, combine the flour, salt, and sugar in a food processor. Add the butter and process until the mixture resembles coarse meal. With the machine running, add the water 1 tablespoon at a time; the dough will pull away from the sides of the processor.

On a lightly floured work surface, form the dough into a ball. Flatten into a disk, cover in plastic wrap, and refrigerate for 30 minutes.

To make the filling, combine the cranberries, water, and $\frac{1}{2}$ of the cup sugar in small saucepan. Bring to a boil, reduce the heat to medium-high, and cook, stirring occasionally, for 15 minutes, or until thickened. Remove from the heat and let cool completely.

In a large bowl, combine the remaining 1 cup sugar, the eggs, mascarpone, and mango juice. Stir until smooth. Force the mixture through a sieve into another large bowl, using the back of a large spoon. Stir in the cranberry mixture until well blended.

Preheat the oven to 350 F.

On a floured work surface, roll out the dough $\frac{1}{4}$-inch thick. Lay the dough in a 9-inch tart pan, allowing the sides to rise $\frac{1}{4}$ inch above the rim. Prick a few holes in the dough and line with parchment paper. Fill with rice and bake for 15 minutes, or until set. Remove the paper and rice. Pour the filling into the tart shell and bake 30 to 35 minutes, or until the filling is just set. Let cool, then refrigerate the tart until firm, at least 1 hour. Serve with fresh whipped cream.

Serves 8

Cranberry Apple Pie

Cranberries add color and a sweet-tart flavor to that American favorite, apple pie.

Pie Pastry

    $2 \frac{1}{4}$ cups all-purpose flour

    $\frac{1}{2}$ teaspoon salt

    1 tablespoon sugar

    $\frac{1}{2}$ cup (1 stick) unsalted butter, cut into small pieces

    $\frac{1}{3}$ cup vegetable shortening

    6 tablespoons ice water

Filling

    $2 \frac{1}{2}$ cups cranberries, coarsely chopped

    5 large Granny Smith apples, peeled, cored, and thinly sliced

    2 cups sugar

    $\frac{1}{4}$ cup apple cider

    $\frac{1}{2}$ teaspoon vanilla extract

    3 tablespoons all-purpose flour

    1 egg beaten with 1 tablespoon milk

To make the pastry, combine the flour, salt, and sugar in a food processor. Pulse to blend. Add the butter and shortening and pulse until the mixture resembles coarse meal. Add the ice water 1 table-spoon at a time, pulsing to incorporate. Continue until the dough begins to pull together. On a lightly floured surface, form the dough into a ball. Divide in half and form into 2 disks. Wrap in plastic wrap and refrigerate for 30 minutes.

Preheat the oven to 350 F. To make the filling, combine the cranberries, apples, sugar, apple cider, vanilla, and flour in a large bowl. Stir to blend. On a lightly floured surface, roll out one disk of dough $\frac{1}{8}$ inch thick. Fit the dough into a 9-inch deep dish pie plate, allowing the excess to hang over the edge. Spoon in the filling, including any juice. Roll out the second disk of dough $\frac{1}{8}$ inch thick. Cover the pie with top crust. Trim the edges, crimp, and pierce the top with a knife to make vents. Brush the egg mixture over the top crust.

Bake for 1 hour, or until the pastry is nicely browned and the juices are boiling through the vents. Let cool on a wire rack 30 minutes before serving.

Serves 8

Cranberry Turnovers

Nearly any fruit can be used in a turnover—it's a versatile dessert. With the perfect balance of sweet and a hint of sour, these turnovers are proof that cranberries needn't be just a holiday side dish.

4 cups fresh or frozen cranberries
$\frac{1}{4}$ cup cranberry juice or water
1 cup sugar, plus additional for sprinkling
$\frac{1}{2}$ teaspoon vanilla extract
1 tablespoon cornstarch mixed with 2 tablespoons water
2 sheets thawed frozen puff pastry
1 egg, beaten lightly
Vanilla ice cream or whipped cream, for serving

In a large saucepan, combine the cranberries, juice, 1 cup of the sugar, and the vanilla. Cook, stirring occasionally, over medium heat for 15 minutes, or until thickened. Increase the heat to medium-high. Stir in the cornstarch mixture and cook for 1 minute, stirring. Remove from the heat and let cool completely. (For faster cooling, set the pan in an ice bath.)

Preheat the oven to 400 F. Line a baking sheet with parchment paper. On a lightly floured work surface, roll the pastry out $\frac{1}{8}$ inch thick. Cut each sheet into 4 squares. Working with one pastry square at a time, brush the egg around the edge. Spoon $\frac{1}{4}$ cup cranberry filling into the center of a round and fold dough over to make a triangle. Seal the edges tightly by crimping with a fork. Place on the prepared pan. Repeat the process with remaining pastry squares and filling. Refrigerate the turnovers for 10 minutes, or until firm. Remove from the refrigerator and brush the tops with the remaining egg. With a sharp knife, make 3 diagonal 1-inch cuts in the top of each turnover. Sprinkle with sugar. Bake for 20 to 25 minutes, or until golden. Transfer to wire racks to cool slightly. Serve warm, with vanilla ice cream or whipped cream.

Makes 8 turnovers

Cranberry-Pear Crumble

This dessert is quick and easy to prepare.

Crumb Topping

> 1 cup all-purpose flour
>
> $\frac{1}{2}$ cup firmly packed brown sugar
>
> $\frac{1}{4}$ cup granulated sugar
>
> $\frac{1}{2}$ teaspoon ground cinnamon
>
> Pinch of salt
>
> $\frac{1}{2}$ cup (1 stick) unsalted butter, at room temperature

Crumble Filling

> 2 cups fresh or frozen cranberries
>
> 4 large Bosc pears, peeled, cored, and coarsely chopped
>
> $\frac{3}{4}$ cup granulated sugar
>
> 2 tablespoons all-purpose flour
>
> Vanilla ice cream or whipped cream, for serving

Preheat the oven to 350 F. Butter an 8 by 8-inch baking dish.

To make the topping, combine the flour, brown sugar, sugar, cinnamon, and salt in a medium bowl. Stir to blend. Using your fingers, rub in butter until the mixture is crumbly. Refrigerate for 10 minutes.

To make the filling, combine the cranberries, pears, sugar, and flour in a large bowl. Stir to blend. Pour the filling into the prepared baking dish. Sprinkle the topping evenly over the fruit and bake for 50 minutes, or until bubbling and golden brown.

Serves 6 to 8

Drenched Cranberry Cake

This is one of my favorite desserts. Not only is it incredibly easy to make, it's unbelievably good.

2 cups all-purpose flour

1 cup sugar

2 $\frac{1}{2}$ teaspoons baking powder

3 tablespoons vegetable shortening, melted

$\frac{2}{3}$ cup milk

1 egg

2 cups fresh or frozen cranberries

Sauce

$\frac{1}{2}$ cup (1 stick) unsalted butter

1 cup sugar

$\frac{3}{4}$ cup heavy cream

$\frac{1}{2}$ vanilla bean, split lengthwise

Preheat the oven to 350 F. Butter a 9-inch round pan.

Sift the flour, sugar, and baking powder into a large bowl. Add the shortening, milk, and egg. Beat for 2 minutes, or until smooth. Stir in the cranberries. Pour into the prepared pan, smooth the top, and bake for 1 hour, or until an inserted toothpick comes out clean. Transfer to a wire rack.

While the cake is baking, make the sauce: Melt the butter in the top of a double boiler over simmering water. Add the sugar, cream, and vanilla bean. Stir to mix well. Cook, stirring occasionally, for 5 minutes. Remove the vanilla bean. Serve the cake with each individual slice generously topped with the warmed sauce.

Serves 8

Indian Pudding with Cranberry Ice Cream

The combination of cornmeal and cranberries in this dessert conjures up images of colonial New England.

Cranberry Ice Cream

    1 cup fresh or frozen cranberries

    $^1/_4$ cup granulated sugar

    $^1/_4$ cup water

    1 pint good-quality ice cream, slightly softened

Indian Pudding

    3 cups milk

    $^1/_2$ cup yellow cornmeal

    $^1/_2$ teaspoon salt

    2 tablespoons unsalted butter

    2 eggs

    $^1/_4$ cup firmly packed dark brown sugar

    1 tablespoon molasses

    $^1/_4$ cup maple syrup

    $^1/_4$ teaspoon freshly grated nutmeg

To make the ice cream, combine the cranberries, sugar, and water in a small saucepan. Bring to a boil over high heat. Reduce the heat to medium and simmer, stirring frequently for 10 minutes. Remove from the heat and let cool completely. Put the ice cream in a medium bowl. Add the cranberry mixture and stir well to blend. Freeze for 1 hour, or until hard.

To make the pudding, preheat the oven to 350 F. Lightly spray an 8-inch square baking dish with vegetable-oil cooking spray. Pour the milk into a medium, heavy saucepan. Sprinkle the cornmeal and salt into the milk, whisking constantly. Bring to a boil over medium-high heat, stirring constantly. Reduce the heat to medium and simmer for 10 minutes, stirring constantly, until thick and creamy. Remove from the heat, whisk in the butter, and let cool for 10 minutes.

In a large bowl, combine the eggs, brown sugar, molasses, maple syrup, and nutmeg. Whisk well to blend. Gradually stir in the cornmeal mixture. Pour the batter into the prepared dish and smooth the top. Place the dish in a large baking pan and add water to the pan to come halfway up the sides of the dish. Bake for 1 hour and 45 minutes, or until set. Serve with the cranberry ice cream.

Serves 6

Oatmeal Cranberry Cookies with Chocolate Chips

The chocolate chips can be replaced with pecans, walnuts, or macadamia nuts. The dough will keep, covered, in the refrigerator for several weeks.

$1/2$ cup (1 stick) unsalted butter, at room temperature

1 cup firmly packed brown sugar

1 egg

$1/2$ teaspoon vanilla extract

$1/4$ teaspoon salt

1 cup all-purpose flour

$1/2$ teaspoon baking powder

$1/2$ teaspoon baking soda

$1/4$ cup quick-cooking rolled oats

$1/2$ cup dried cranberries

$1/2$ cup chocolate chips

Preheat the oven to 350 F. In a large bowl, beat the butter and sugar together until light and fluffy. Add the egg and vanilla, and beat to combine. In a medium bowl, combine the salt, flour, baking powder, baking soda, and oats. Stir well to blend.

Add the dry ingredients to the wet ingredients and stir to blend. Stir in the cranberries and chocolate chips. Drop by rounded tablespoonfuls onto an ungreased baking sheet 1 $\frac{1}{2}$ inches apart. Bake for 12 to 15 minutes, or until golden. Let cool for 1 minute on the baking sheet, then transfer to wire rack.

Makes 24 cookies

About the Author

Jennifer Trainer Thompson is an accomplished cook,
a James Beard Award nominee, and author or coauthor of seven cookbooks
and two nonfiction books. Her articles have appeared in the
New York Times, Travel & Leisure, Diversion, Omni, *and* Harvard.
Thompson is the owner and chef of the Jump Up & Kiss Me brand of food products
(including hot sauces) and prolific Ten Speed poster producer.
Thompson lives with her family in rural Massachusetts.